CLINICALLY LICENSED
NOW WHAT...

CLINICALLY LICENSED
NOW WHAT...

A SIMPLE GUIDE TO STARTING
PRIVATE PRACTICE

LAKEYSHA WARD, LPC-S

Charleston, SC
www.PalmettoPublishing.com

Clinically licensed now what...

Copyright © 2023 by Lakeysha Ward, LPC-S

All rights reserved.

No portion of this book may be reproduced, stored in a retrieval system, or transmitted in any form by any means–electronic, mechanical, photocopy, recording, or other–except for brief quotations in printed reviews, without prior permission of the author.

First Edition

Paperback ISBN: 9798822921894
eBook ISBN: 9798822921900

To my beautiful wife for all the help and support with writing this book. To all of my friends and family who encouraged me to write this book, thank you for all of your support. It has always been told to me that I am a great teacher and possess a lot of knowledge when it comes to being a clinician so I felt the need to share the information I have to hopefully help others in starting their private practice.

■ ■ ■

TABLE OF CONTENTS

Prologue ix

Chapter 1   Things to consider..........................13
Chapter 2   Where to begin..............................16
Chapter 3   Self Care...................................19
Chapter 4   Sole proprietor versus LLC..................23
Chapter 5   Group versus individual private practice....30
Chapter 6   Office versus virtual.......................35
Chapter 7   HIPAA compliant platforms for
            documentation...............................38
Chapter 8   Forms.......................................41
Chapter 9   Where are my clients going to come from?....45
Chapter 10 Billing system and being able to keep track...49

Resources 53

PROLOGUE

Congratulations on completing all requirements needed to obtain your licensure to practice as an unsupervised clinician. BREATHE.... Bask in the accomplishments that you have achieved with getting your licensure. This is a great task to accomplish and has taken time, perseverance and consistency. There were many of days and nights, that I wanted to give up however without consistency and perseverance we would accomplish nothing. If you are anything like myself, I was one of those people that obtained my licensure and was on to the next life goal. For me sitting still causes boredom and boredom leads to nothingness. Therefore, let's get into starting your own private practice.

First off, let me start by saying this will not be your typical boring instructional book because I, Lakeysha, am not a boring person or instructor. So, prepare yourself for some humor, some off the wall commentary and good knowledge that will help you get the ball to rolling. This book is a starter that has the fundamental information to help guide you through the process of what your next step is if you desire to start your own private practice. By no means is this a step-by-step guide. Think of this book as the ground work on how to proceed. This is a general overview of what you will need and the common things you will need in order to begin your own private practice journey.

When I obtained my license, I started packing up my home to prepare to relocate to either Texas or Georgia. Living in Memphis, TN was not going to get me the financial stability I was seeking nor the lifestyle I craved. I begin filling out applications in both states. Due to owning my home, I had to determined what salary requirements I needed in order to float my current lifestyle and coverage my mortgage if my renters were not paying or if I did not have renters.

I don't think I took the time to really sit with the accomplishment because I knew my worth and I was not obtaining it while staying in Memphis. If you have the ability to do so, sit and recognize all of your hard work, dedication and self-motivation that you have achieved. Often times we don't realize all that we have done and all the roles that we have been juggling while completing the criteria to meet licensure. So now that we have taken that really short moment of self-recognition, I am sure you are contemplating what is next and where do I begin? If you are not already working in your field this is a major life question. If you have been working in your field the decision might be slightly easier however life decisions tend to be difficult to make for some. I suggest listing your options, your pros and cons to those options and see which weighs more to you.

Reading this book is a great starting point to gain the knowledge of what it will take to start your own private practice. I was lucky to have experienced multiple counseling fields while in undergrad, graduate school, practicum, internship and clinical hours. I have experience with adolescents and adults in the following fields: drugs and alcohol, mental health (anything diagnostic), behavioral health (behavioral modification type counseling such as ABA therapy for children with autism), inpatient and outpatient psychiatric hospitals, group therapy, individual and family therapy. I started my career with adolescent (12-17 yrs. old) male sex offenders. I know, I know go ahead and cringe, most people do when I tell them about this population and answer the multiple questions. Having this vast amount of experience has allowed for me to strengthen my clinical skills. Keep in mind, yes mental and behavioral health have now become the same thing but back when I started this journey it was separate by name.

When I started my private practice journey, I had no clue where to begin and literally no help in figuring it out. I searched the internet for answers, keep in mind I have been in this field for over 16 years. I became licensed in Tennessee in 2014 and licensed in Texas in 2015. I am writing this book to help others avoid doing it alone as well as doing it the hard way which is unguided. Luckily, I have experience, personally and professional, in helping guide people when they are not certain what to do next if they desire to start their own private practice.

CHAPTER 1

THINGS TO CONSIDER

- Target population
- Type of sessions (groups, individual and/or couples)
- Age range (children, adolescents, adults and/or elderly)

Are you asking yourself what do I do now since I have my clinical licensure? Well as a Licensed Professional Counselor (LPC) you have multiple options such as inpatient/outpatient mental/behavioral health settings, case management, insurance companies, residential facilities and acute psychiatric hospitals so on and so forth. Licensed Clinical Social Workers (LCSW) have the options above in addition to the medical fields.

In the beginning, I was not really sure of what population, age range and type of sessions I desired to work with however I advise you get as much experience as you can in multiple areas of behavioral health. Population refers to chemical dependency, mental health, marriage/family and LBGTQ+. Type of session refers to individual, group, marriage and family. You also need to think about the age groups you would prefer to work with such as children, adolescents, young adults and older adults. I have had associates say "I only want to work with kids" etc. Being this specific could limit your clientele to just one area hence the reason I sought out as many different areas of the counseling field while in college. In my private practice, I started out with no limitations and as it grew, I began to limit the population and age group that I would accept. When you think of private practice, this is your own business and you control who you accept or decline.

Next question you have to ask yourself is what age group do you desire to work with such as adults, adolescents, or kids? The age rang for children is under 12yrs old and adolescents range from 12-18. Adolescents were a learning curve for me especially with the population that struggled with alcohol and drugs (now referred to as chemical dependence). When accepting adolescents, there is the consideration of possible legal challenges. One parent might be on board with counseling while the other is not. This is a legal nightmare however obtaining proper written consents from both parents is a must regardless if they are in agreement or not. Both parents, if in the adolescents' life, need to sign consent forms even if they are married. Better to be safe than sorry, more documentation versus not enough is the best motto to live by.

What type of counseling sessions do you feel well versed in or want to explore such as marriage/family, individual or group. These can also be broken down into more specifics such as depression/anxiety, personality disorders, marital/relationship issues, child development, eating disorder, sex, grief, art, and music therapy. Keep in mind the term therapy and counseling are interchangeable. If you feel more passionate about a specific population and type of session, go for that however don't limit yourself to just that population and type of session. Market yourself for those two things but also include other areas you have received training and supervision in. Later, we will go further into more marketing details. I am a strong believer that if you are too strict with your limitation, this could potentially stifle your growth as a clinician. Some have been highly successful in just focusing on one specific population and type of session. This has also been a complication for some when expanding their cliental in private practice. Knowing who you are and what your niche is as a clinician is an essential part of your success as a licensed clinician.

CHAPTER 2:

WHERE TO BEGIN

- NPI
- Name of business
- Tax ID/EIN

Let's walk through the initial first steps to starting your own professional identity. The first three steps will not be time consuming or stressful however please make sure you are paying attention to the information you are inputting on both applications. The majority of the steps will have to be done simultaneously.

Your first step is to obtain a National Provider Identification number aka NPI. Why do you need an NPI? Well, a couple of reasons: This number is a unique government-issued identifier for healthcare professionals to help identify who you are as a provider. Secondly, your NPI is needed to file claims with insurance companies as well as set you apart from other professionals in your field even if you decide to only engage in self-pay clients. How do you get this number? Is there a cost to do so because maybe your funds are limited?

Applying for your NPI is free and easy! To obtain your NPI, apply online visit the National Plan and Provider Enumeration System (NPPES) website, https://nppes.cms.hhs.gov/#/. This is the first step to setting yourself up as a professionally licensed clinician outside of obtaining your actual license. When applying for this make sure to make your home address private. This information that you put on your application for your NPI will be on the world wide web for all to see so make sure you're not putting your personal address as public.

Before applying for your EIN, think of the name of your business. This will be needed to apply for your EIN correctly which we will get to shortly. When you think of a business name, keep in mind this will be on the forefront of what service you provide. I could not come up with something cleaver so I took my last name and counseling which lead to **Ward Counseling**. Also, when thinking of a business name, ask yourself will your potential clientele know what service you offer by this name? You can apply for a Doing Business As (DBA) or your Limited Liability Corporation (LLC) with your local secretary of state office. We will go over the difference for both in a later chapter.

The next most important thing you will need to apply for is your Employer identification number aka EIN or Tax ID. This number is highly imperative if you desire to start your own private practice and you are accepting insurance payments. This number is required for credentialing with the insurance companies and used for billing the insurance companies. You can apply for this number through the IRS.gov website https://www.irs.gov/businesses/small-businesses-self-employed/how-to-apply-for-an-ein.

Again, if you're asking if there is a cost, no there is not a fee i.e., it's free! The goal is to help you setup your business in a cost-efficient capacity. I believe in the overhead being as low as possible because I like to make more profit from what I do versus shoveling out my hard-earned coins. Obtain your NPI before applying for your EIN. Doing it this way will help decrease the overwhelming anxiety you may have as well as making the rest of the process go smoother.

CHAPTER 3:

SELF CARE

- How to take care of yourself
- Suggestions on self-care
- Prevent burnout

In the meantime, while waiting on those numbers, let's implement some self-care. I learned the hard way that clinicians tend to be the worst at caring for themselves the first few years of their careers. I'd became overwhelmed, stressed and was not properly caring for myself when I was at my first job fresh out of undergrad. I was working with adolescent sexual offenders which was great, fulfilling and rewarding however with the stressors of the job along with my personal life, they both took a toll on my physical well-being. I thought I had an aneurysm or a brain tumor. Did all the medical test to rule it out. Nothing was found except stress. YIKES!!!! Yes, stress is a booger bear to the body when not managed appropriately. I was taken off work for 2 weeks, given medication to sleep and help with the neck pain. When told it was stress, I did a self-reflection and vowed to myself that I will never not take care of myself first. Yup, I used a double negative because it was a terrible amount of stress and it would never occur again. In order to be the best clinician to your clients it is crucial to take care of yourself first to avoid physical, mental, medical symptomology as well as burnout. In a Counseling today article entitled "Taking care of yourself as a counselor by Lynne Shallcross", January 17, 2011, she discusses the importance of taking care of yourself. The following is an excerpt from the article mentioned above:

> "Counselors who neglect their own mental, physical and spiritual self-care eventually run out of 'oxygen' and cannot effectively help their clients because all of their energy is going out to the clients and nothing is coming back in to replenish the counselors' energy.", Shallcross, January 17, 2011.

I am stopping the instructional and encouraging you to implement one or more of the following self-care suggestions. As mentioned above, we tend to not take very good care of ourselves. We as humans, do not like change regardless if it is good or bad. At times, changing our daily routine can impact us in several ways we are not even aware of. I have included several self-care suggestions in attempts to help with decreasing the overwhelming feelings you might be having and encouraging you to get into the practice of self-care. Taking care of yourself is not selfish. I always tell people if I don't take care of myself on a regular basis, I cannot take care of others regardless if it's personal or professional. A few things to try are:

- **Exercise**- burns off that stress
- **Vacation** (big or small)- takes you away from the stressors and refreshes you to begin again
- **Read a book that has nothing to do with your normal life**- escape into someone else's world
- **Soothing bath**-relaxes your muscles and soothes you
- **Listen to favorite soothing music**- as a clinician music is therapeutic
- **Be social with friends and family, if this is not your norm**- socializing for some can relieve daily stress because it has nothing to do with the work life or daily life stressors. Surround yourself with positive people. DO NOT give therapeutic advice during these socializing sessions lol
- **Play games**- return to fun time
- **Meditate/Yoga**- helps center your mind, learn to control your thought processes and slows down those thoughts
- **Massage**- releases toxins, relaxing and rejuvenating

Burnout is the greatest enemy within the counseling field. We are focused on taking care of others however not so much ourselves. When you begin to feel the burnout, it is already too late however you can prevent this by taking care of yourself on a frequent basis. Learn to take care of you, before taking care of others.

CHAPTER 4:

SOLE PROPRIETOR VERSUS LLC

- Sole proprietor
- LLC
- Incorporated vs Corporated

In this chapter, we will go over the simplistic differences between sole proprietor (DBA) and LLC. The next decision is how you want to file your new private practice, meaning do you want to do a Sole Proprietor/DBA (doing business as) or LLC (Limited Liability Company). This decision needs to be made at the same time you are applying for your EIN.

Ward Counseling is a sole proprietor because I knew I would never expand my practice to have more than just myself. Sole proprietor, basically means you are responsible for everything financial that occurs with your business. If the business goes bankrupt, so do you. Calm down and breath, it sounds worse than what it really is. The professional liability insurance you required to have and maintain will cover legal matters. When you file your personal taxes, your private practice taxes will be included. Sole proprietorships do not produce a separate business entity. This means your business assets and liabilities are not separate from your personal assets and liabilities. You can be held personally liable for the debts and obligations of the business. For example: if you work at a full-time job (W2 job) and have your own private practice (1099 contractor) you will file both of those together.

The following charts were taken from Legalzoom.com.

SOLE PROPRIETOR

Better if you need an easy set-up	You're personally on the hook for business liabilities	No personal liability protection
No paperwork to start; you may still need a **DBA** or business licenses to operate legally	Taxed once—you pay on profits in your personal tax return	
One owner max	Less hassle; separate tax return not needed	

Sole proprietor will require a DBA. This DBA is easy to obtain through the Secretary of State office in your local city. This DBA can last up to last 10 yrs. There are two other forms of business however they typically do not apply to private practice unless you are planning to build an entire corporation so those two will not be discussed. Please make sure to verify and check with your local Secretary of State office because some states may have different requirements for DBA. The information above is for Texas.

Sole proprietorship is good for low-risk business such as private practice. Having your own private practice with your professional liability insurance is very low risk especially if you are following the laws and ethics of your license. If you are planning to accept insurance, having liability insurance is a must and not optional. I do not advise practicing without professional liability insurance regardless if you accept insurance or not because it leaves you completely open for financial distress if anyone desires to sue you.

A Limited Liability Company aka LLC agency, gives you more tax breaks and write off opportunities. The cost of starting an LLC is much higher than a Sole proprietor/DBA. Please review the chart below for the pros and cons for both.

LIMITED LIABILITY COMPANY

Better for max flexibility in how you manage and run your business; board of directors not required	You're *not* personally on the hook for business liabilities	Ongoing filings and fees to stay in compliance
Unlimited owners (aka "members") allowed	Taxed once or twice; you're free to choose which can help minimize taxes	LLCs can't go public
		Not recognized globally; you may be taxed as a corporation in other countries

There are minor differences between the two however the major difference is that LLC has the potential for multiple owners and you don't have personal liability. LLCs are good for high-risk businesses that desire to protect their personal assets. If the private practice goes bankrupt, you are not personally responsible for that financial loss. As a Sole proprietor, you take full responsibility for your business. Example of LLC: if someone sues you, your personal home, car, savings account etc. are not impacted and cannot be touched in the lawsuit. With sole proprietorship if someone sues you, everything is up for grabs i.e., your car, home, office etc. Do not let this frighten you because that is why you have liability insurance. I utilize HIPSO which is highly affordable and has discounts for students as well as new licensees. HIPSO is a professional liability insurance that will protect you and again is required by insurance panels. You are able to find the link in the resource section at the back of this book.

With an LLC, you will be responsible for paying Medicare and social security taxes due to being self-employed even if your private practice is a part time job, you still have to pay a percentage of your profits to the government due to co-pays and insurance reimbursements not being taxed. Recent research regarding incorporated and corporated, it seems as though it aligns with DBA and LLC.

For some, the panic will set in due to thinking of the worst-case scenario. Being in business on your own can be stressful however this is the reason you obtain the liability insurance to protect yourself and your business, regardless if it will be sole proprietorship or limited liability corporation.

Simply put, incorporated is separate from business owner and has its own set of nuances. Unincorporated is the same as the business owner, you basically are your business. I am Ward Counseling and vice versa. If a person sues Ward Counseling, they are suing me as well. Again, the cost of starting a sole proprietorship is significantly less than LLC. When you are thinking about taxes, both your DBA and personal taxes will be filed together with special business owner write offs. Make sure to keep track of the things you purchase for your office space and general private practice such as furniture, supplies etc.

With an LLC, you will file the business taxes separately than your personal taxes. If you hold a job that provides you with a W2 or takes taxes out of your weekly/biweekly check, you will still get business write offs. I advise obtaining a CPA or a well-versed tax professional to maximize your tax benefits.

CHAPTER 5:

GROUP VERSUS INDIVIDUAL PRIVATE PRACTICE

- Group
- Individual
- Pros/Cons

Now that you have your NPI, Tax ID/EIN and business name/identification, let's talk about the differences between group and individual private practice. Initially, I started out with a group practice. With a group practice you will not need to obtain your own Tax ID/EIN because the group utilizes its own Tax ID/EIN however you will still need your NPI number.

Pros of joining a group practice are: they typically get you credentialed on insurance panels. This is a plus especially if you personally do not want to deal with the credentialing process which has definitely started to become easier since I completed the process. I had stacks and stacks of applications that had the same repetitive information. I questioned the reason the insurance companies had not went electronic with their credentialing applications however most if not all have, thankfully.

Group practice handles the billing and managing of co-pays for your clients. So, this eliminates you having to personally file the claims or keep up with copays and insurance information. Some group practices control scheduling and paperwork as well. This prevents you from having to worry if you have all the proper consents to protect yourself as well as not having to keep up with your schedule. Due to you providing the group with your availability, you typically only have to keep up with what days you have clients scheduled.

Initially, joining a group practice allowed me to be free to solely focus on therapy and get the experience of having private practice clients. At times you are not able to screen the inquires of those individuals seeking to start therapy before the initial session. Depending on the clinician, this might be seen as either a pro or con. Some group practices ask you for your desired population, the diagnosis you prefer to work with and age groups.

A potential con in a group practice is that you are paid a percentage of what is earned from each session. A year was spent with the group practice and I enjoyed that setting. I suggest starting out in group practice to get your feet wet as well as figure out what you desire to do and if owning your own private practice is something that you desire to undertake.

After being in the group practice for one year, an opportunity landed in my lap and I took it. I was gifted (allowed to sublease) an office from a coworker and close friend. That sublet eventually became my own leased office. That clinician allowed me to utilize her office manager in regards to billing and scheduling which was a great asset to have because I had no clue on how to bill or where to begin. I took it upon myself to get credentialed under my own tax ID/EIN. As previously mentioned, most insurance companies have gone to electronic credentialing applications. Information on credentialing will be discussed in the upcoming chapters.

The number one pro to owning your own private practice is you obtain all the profits from the sessions which is a major plus for the majority of clinicians. Secondary pro, is that you have more control over your scheduling which allows you to screen who you will accept or decline due to appropriate fit. Cons for some are having to keep up with the billing, with the schedule and reaching out to clients for their appointments. I utilize a documentation system that has that ability to file your claim, connect the client's insurance and keep track of scheduling if you desire to pay for a slightly higher fee for the aforementioned capabilities. Documentation will be discussed in detail in a later chapter. I like to focus on being accessible to my clients, so sending a quick appointment confirmation text takes less than a minute out of my day. I can ensure the reminder was sent in a 24-hour period, which for me allows confirmation or cancellation to prepare for the next day. I have a mindset that if my overhead is costing more than what I am profiting, there has to be a change.

The question has been asked, how to transition from group to individual private practice? It is overwhelming at the beginning, however starting your own business can be just as overwhelming as when you started with the group practice. You might be questioning, what happens with your current group private practice clients when or if you move to your own individual private practice? The professional way to transition your clients from group to your own private practice is by informing the clients at the group practice that you will no longer be practicing with the group and you have started your own private practice. Informing your group clients that they have the option to stay with the group practice but would be transferred to another clinician or continue counseling in your own private practice. This can only be done effectively if there isn't a noncompete clause in your contract with the group practice if you decide to go that route. Informing them that they would be transferred to another clinician in the event they desired to stay with the group practice, allows the client to make an informed decision. Most of my clients transitioned out of the group practice to my practice. I would be remiss if I failed to mention, it would be beneficial for you to review your contract with your group practice prior to resignation, as this should inform you of your options for transferring clients, resignation time etc.

Starting therapy takes a lot of courage. You will come to find that once a client is with you and you all gain a healthy rapport, they will be willing to continue the therapeutic relationship that has been formed. Don't panic about continuing to obtain new clients, they are plentiful especially due to the current state of the overall society.

CHAPTER 6:

OFFICE VERSUS VIRTUAL

- Office
- Virtual

This is one of those areas that you will have to get a feel for. If you decide to obtain an office lease, here are some questions to ask yourself:

- Is the office located in a convenient area?
- Is it located on a main line of public transportation?
- Is the office handicap/physically accessible?
- Is parking plentiful and/or connected to other businesses?
- Is your office private enough to allow confidentiality?
- Is furniture and office equipment provided in your rent?

When thinking about the population you serve you may have to think about more than the above questions however those are the basic questions to ask yourself when choosing an office space and in-person sessions. Some clients will prefer to be physically present which could be for multiple reasons such as level of comfort, privacy issues and potentially helping to have a break from the environment that could be creating the symptoms the client is seeking therapy for.

The positives of telehealth are that you can reach a larger clientele in the state your licensed in versus those individuals in the local area of the office. This also gives you the ability to see clients that are not physically capable of attending sessions. When I think about the numerous clients that have the fear of being stigmatized due to attending therapy, telehealth has been a positive change for them. They are able to meet with a therapist in the comfort of their own home or environment without questioning if someone they knew would see them going into a therapist office. This causes stress on clients which leads to avoiding seeking help from a clinician. Typically, the initial reason for getting into this field is to help others with mental health, however when we think about people that can or are willing to obtain the guidance from a clinician this is a small population for multiple reasons.

You will have to determine which is better for you. I suggest trying both to get a feel for them each because they both have their advantages and disadvantages. As mentioned above, having an office gives you the ability to read body language which includes facial expression and body shifting. It will allow you to pick up on nervous ticks a person might have as well as potentially determining certain tells that the person is uncomfortable, potentially not being fully honest with you or even feeling comfortable with you. Completing sessions via virtual telehealth you can read the facial language along with the verbal to potentially pick on clues that will be helpful to you and client in gaining rapport.

CHAPTER 7:

HIPAA COMPLIANT PLATFORMS FOR DOCUMENTATION

I have utilized Simple Practice since starting my practice. This platform provides you with the ability to keep secure documentation, forms that can be utilized and a video chat platform that is HIPAA compliant. They provide a few options depending on your range of cost. The starter package is affordable but provides you with the basics, which include client roster, self-filled treatment plan and DAP or SOAP format note. The essential package allows you to utilize the telehealth feature Simple practice provides that is compliant along with appointment reminders and much more. The Plus package gives you all access to Wiley treatment plans, telehealth, appointment reminders and insurance billing.

Website link to simple practice: https://www.simplepractice.com/pricing/.

For me, I tend to only utilize the minor functions just for documentation purposes. As I have stated many times already, I prefer to keep my overhead low as possible to increase my profits. However, your ability to maintain billing, sending appointment reminders and creating a treatment plan will determine which package will be more beneficial for your practice needs. There are other platforms but I am not well versed with the others. Listed below are four other platforms you can utilize, look at all resources and compare them to see which one meets your needs.

Again, I have only utilized simple practice and would not have specifics on other platforms. Therapy notes (www.therapynotes.com) starts at $49 per month for solo clinician increasing to $59 per month for 30 or more users. Power diary (https://www.powerdiary.com/us/profession/mental-health-software/) is another platform that provides several options however I did not like the pricing which is per week ranging from $5 per week to $30 per week. It has multiple features and is HIPAA compliant. The last one that I've come across is sessionshealth.com https://www.sessionshealth.com/ the pricing starts with freemium that is for 1 practitioner up to 3 clients which is free. The other package is $35 unlimited clients and an additional $25per additional practitioner. Theranest is another popular platform https://theranest.com/.

After researching documentation for therapist, I come across www.clinicsource.com that provides templates, and training however this platform is costly if you are just starting your private practice. Sessions.com (www.sessions.com) is a platform that will provide a plethora of resources such as forms, calendar sync and insurance eligibility/coverage. All have the ability to add more therapist if you desire to have clinicians in your practice.

CHAPTER 8:

FORMS

Now that you have picked a secure documentation platform, what paperwork do you need in order to stay compliant? As mentioned in Chapter 7, most platforms will provide forms and documentation templates. However, depending on how elaborate you desire your intake packet to be, will determine the information you will put in it. To start off your intake packet, introduce yourself to your clients which should include name of practice, how long you have been licensed, your clinical experience and what therapy modalities you specialize in along with certifications. Make sure to put the complaint contact information which can be found on your state boards website. You can even post the complaint information in your office and on your website. The next area is what services you provide such as individual, group, couples and/or marital counseling.

Discuss what to expect in psychotherapy which includes how you conduct your first few sessions, encourage the client to evaluate the first few sessions, and your philosophy on the therapy journey. Some clients think that one or two sessions will resolve the issue and this is far from the truth. Educate your client about the time commitment, financial commitment and the most important "therapy is what you put in to it. If you put in half the effort, you will make half progress however if you put in 100% effort then you will see 100% progress" (Lakeysha Ward, LPC-S).

Discuss the expectations of therapy and what that looks like typically. This is the verbiage utilized in my intake packet:

> "A 45–60-minute session will be scheduled as needed, the duration and length between appointments will fluctuate throughout treatment as needed. Once an appointment is scheduled, you are responsible for all fees pertaining to this session, unless you provide a 24-hour advance notice of cancellation or re-schedule (unless both you and I agree that you are unable to attend due to circumstances beyond your control). Treatment can last up to 6 months or greater. Sessions are scheduled in a progression, beginning once a week, transitioning to every 2 weeks, every 3 weeks and then once

> per month. Scheduling is easily adjusted per individual needs."

This will help your client (s) who have not had therapy become aware of what therapy will look like.

Your next section is confidentiality. This portion is highly important to include in the intake packet because it will serve as a legal documentation that they have read this information. However, I advise verbally reviewing the confidentiality in the initial session and document this in your note. There have been several clinicians come to me noting their clients complain that they were not aware of the confidentiality and limitations of therapy despite them signing or initialing it.

Your next section is how to contact you and your after-hour service if applicable. Best practice with returning calls, emails or any other message is to respond in a 24-hour period. There are some clinicians who fail to respond which discourages clients from the therapeutic process.

Professional fee agreement, this is important to be able to tell your client their copay prior to session. Obtain the insurance information to determine eligibility and benefits prior to initial session. This process can be completed through availity.com, headway or calling the persons insurance. Availity is a free billing system that gives free access to several insurance companies. It allows you to check insurance benefits, file your claim, track it, obtain payment disbursement and the system is fairly easy to navigate. Headway is free to providers. This system gets you credentialed, takes the clients co-pay and pays you for each session.

Next section is about the client, which includes demographics such as: name, age, date of birth, employment statues, marital status, children, medical/ mental health diagnosis, medications and emergency contact. Other sections can consist of the reason for seeking therapy, past abuse/ trauma, alcohol and drug use, suicidal/homicidal ideation/ attempt history and inquire about past therapy or treatment history. Asking if the client has any fears or concerns about starting therapy is helpful because it can give the clinician insight to fears and thoughts about therapy. This can help start a conversation with your new client due to some clients previously starting therapy but something negative occurring and they ceased therapy.

Release of information form if anyone wants to be able to give you access to discuss with a doctor, spouse etc. include this form as well. If you plan to engage in telehealth therapy, include this form noting the requirements for telehealth sessions such as the home address of where person is located completing the intake just in case member becomes a danger to themselves or others. This form should also include the HIPPA compliant website you will be utilizing to complete sessions.

CHAPTER 9:

WHERE ARE MY CLIENTS GOING TO COME FROM?

- Cash pay
- Insurance
- Advertising

Regardless if you take cash or insurance make sure to open a business checking and/or saving account. Open this account with your EIN and your DBA (doing business as) or the LLC name. This will help with keeping up with your taxes, and will help with providing an account for office expenses. When you file your taxes, it will be imperative to have your write offs prepared and readily available for your tax preparer.

You are also able to apply for business credit cards. If you decide to obtain a business credit card, make sure to research the benefits you will receive, if approved. Think about cash back and travel points given from each card along with the interest rate. Your business accounts can track your spending habits and your write offs which will be easy for you and your tax professional to keep track of.

Cash pay is lovely to have due to not having to worry about insurance claims, denials or reimbursement rates however taking only cash pay could potentially limit your clientele scope depending on the area you practice in and your cash pay rate. True, this is less stressful when it comes to seeing clients however might stifle your growth in private practice. With cash make sure you are taking out 15% to pay quarterly taxes. You can either total up the months to take 15% out each month and pay quarterly taxes to IRS or 15% from each reimbursement and copay. Having a spreadsheet will make this easy to track or some platforms will track this for you.

You may question how will you obtain referrals with cash pay. Well, this will call for a business website, utilizing psychology today profile (http://www.psychologytoday.com), potential advertisement on several platforms and networking. Social media has become a great free resource to promote your business. Please take caution utilizing social media as an advertising platform. Make sure to keep it professional versus personal. Keep in mind people are coming to you for professional help with things that are going on in their life and should not have access to your social media because that is your life. Try to think about what clients and/or potential clients would think if they saw their potential therapist in an unprofessional manner. Boundaries are clearly set.

Accepting both insurance and cash pay clients can build your client caseload. Clients with insurance will outweigh cash pay clients. You do have the ability to implement a sliding scale, personally I do not implement this because that takes more effort on my behalf to figure out the client's income and what they can afford. Getting on insurance panels was previously a tedious process however it has become easily accessible typically through online portals such as Headway and Alma. If you were credentialed through a group practice to get your feet wet, the credentialling process will be easier due to your NPI already being established as a provider. However sometimes this could make it complicated as well if the person at the insurance company is not paying attention to the different EIN numbers. You can be credentialed with several companies EIN and your NPI so no worries if you want to do a side job like Sondermind or Betterhelp plus your private practice.

If you are just starting your practice and did not get credentialed through a group practice first, credentialing will take time, consistency, effort and follow through on your behalf. When completing the credentialing process, it is imperative to never utilize your social security number as a way to identify yourself as a clinical provider, hence the need for your EIN. Utilize your EIN for everything dealing with your private practice, this is your businesses social security number.

Once on insurance panels your referrals will begin to flow without effort. Godaddy (http://www.godaddy.com) is inexpensive, easy to make your own website without prior website development knowledge, gives you the option for your own url, email address and a few other options. Google suit provides business agreements for website, phone number and emails. Make sure to inquire where your referral comes from in the initial session to track how well your advertising tools are working for your business.

Between psychology today platform and insurance panels my client referrals were plentiful. Keep in mind, my private practice is part time so extra advertising is not needed. If you are going to be full time with your private practice, I suggest having psychology today profile, your business website, insurance panels, business cards, social media business account and networking at events. Vistaprint (Vistaprint.com) and Brandcrowd (brandcrowd.com) are two affordable websites you can create your logo, business cards, and apparel.

CHAPTER 10:

BILLING SYSTEM AND BEING ABLE TO KEEP TRACK

Availity, Headway, Alma and insurance websites can be used for billing. In order to keep up with billing, I employ a simple spreadsheet from excel to keep track of billing, copays and client insurance information. This spreadsheet extremely helpful for tracking what has been billed and especially the client's insurance information. This same spreadsheet is able to track my write offs per month which is extremely valuable when filing taxes. At times, when checking if a claim was paid, you will need the client's insurance information handy which for me is easily accessible through a spreadsheet. The spreadsheet is easily accessible on any format i.e., your business email and/or computer.

QuickBooks and Intuit are resources for income expenses, invoicing, payroll management and inventory management. However, they will not help with managing your insurance claims. I don't have experience using either of these however some have found them really useful in their businesses. Ward Counseling is only operated by me which means QuickBooks or Intuit would not be beneficial. Utilize what is best for your needs.

Headway (https://headway.co/for-providers) and Alma (https://helloalma.com/for-providers) are two new billing and credentialing websites. These websites were not around when starting Ward Counseling however, they are very useful and highly recommended. You can utilize both to get on insurance panels with ease. They do all the work, after you have provided them with the essential information to get you credentialed. Headway allows you to store notes. It provides HIPPA compliant video platform and appointment reminders, all at no cost. However, it does not provide templates such as DAP/SOAP or treatment plans.

Now that you have the basics for starting your private practice, I want to wish you the best of luck and encouragement on your success. I hope this guide has provided you with the groundwork in starting your private practice!! Good luck. If you find yourself in need of more information than what this book has provided, please feel free to visit my website at wardcounseling.net for information on scheduling a consultation to discuss any questions or concerns.

THANKS AGAIN FOR PURCHASING THIS BOOK.

∎ ∎ ∎

RESOURCES

Website link to obtain NPI
https://nppes.cms.hhs.gov

Website link to obtain EIN
https://www.irs.gov

Counseling today article
https://ct.counseling.org

Sole proprietor versus LLC information obtained from legal zoom
https://www.legalzoom.com

Website link to godaddy
https://www.godaddy.com

Website link to obtain information for talkspace
https://www.talkspace.com

Website link to obtain information for betterhelp
https://www.betterhelp.com

Website link to obtain more information on simple practice online platform
https://www.simplepractice.com

Website link to obtain more information on sessions health
http://www.sessionshealth.com

Website link to obtain more information on therapy notes
http://therapynotes.com

www.ingramcontent.com/pod-product-compliance
Lightning Source LLC
LaVergne TN
LVHW051924060526
838201LV00062B/4678